# Goal!
## The history of football

By Enrico Pomarico

Illustrations by Fluidofinto

# Intro

Goal! Such a powerful word!

A magic word with the same meaning in every language, the same emotion that unites people of all ages, origins, genders, and beliefs.

A universal word to express joy, satisfaction, and happiness, right after scoring a… goal!

In the English language, a goal is an objective, a target, an aim, an ambition.
In life, as in sports, a goal is the desire to realise a dream, the ultimate purpose of the game.

Let's take a look into the history of the beautiful game, how it was born, how it grew and developed to become what it is today: the most popular of all sports and a great metaphor for life.

## Table of contents

**Intro**	Page 3

**Chapter 1**
**The birth and evolution of the game**	Page 7

**Chapter 2**
**Beyond the pitch: football and society**	Page 41

**Chapter 3**
**Organisations and competitions**	Page 61

**Chapter 4**
**Making history**	Page 99

# Chapter 1

# The birth and evolution of the game

## 1650 BCE
# Pok-Ta-Pok Mesoamerica

Aztec and Maya used to play the Mesoamerican ballgame which was called Pok-Ta-Pok. There are many versions of this sport and its evolution. They used a 4 kg solid rubber ball and it was played as part of ritual events.

## ~ 400 BCE
# Episkyros Ancient Greece

Episkyros means Common Ball; Ancient Greeks had teams of 14 players who could use also hands like in rugby and Gaelic football. This game inspired Roman soldiers who created the Harpastum.

## 300-200 BCE
## Game of Cuju China

The FIFA has recognised that the Chinese game of Cuju was the first ball game played with the feet.

## 600 CE
## Kemari Japan

This game was inspired by the Japanese practice of Kemari where people would stand in a circle passing the ball to each other without dropping the ball on the ground! Reminds you of something? Keepie uppie!

Goal! • © 2023 Enrico Pomarico

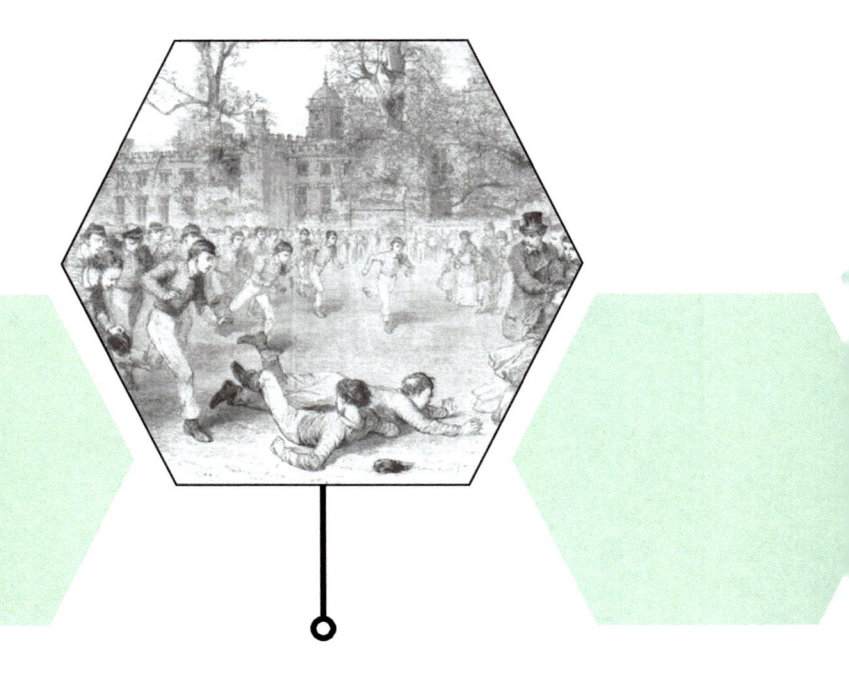

## Middle Ages England

In England's Middle Ages football matches were played town vs town and the teams would include literally **everyone**, the goals could have been 3 miles apart, and a game could have continued during the night and lasted up to 3 days. These games, whose most popular skill was "hacking" (deliberately kicking in the shins), would cause damages, injuries, and death so it was BANNED for a few centuries!

# 1500 CE
# CALCIO STORICO FIORENTINO Italy

Calcio Fiorentino also known as Calcio Storico (Historic Football) was created in Florence, Italy, during the 1500s (the Renaissance era) which was a revival of the Roman games of Harpastum. It was played in the public square and the players were literally fighters than ballers.

Nowadays, the Calcio Storico is still played in Florence once a year as a tournament within the four "quartieri" (neighborhoods) of the city. The feeling of belonging is very strong and players never change color/team: they are Blues, Reds, Whites, or Green forever.

Rules of the game?
27 players each team without substitutes. Mixed martial arts fighting is on until so many players are down so finally a player can try to get the ball in the opponent's net. And when a shot is missed there is a half point awarded to the opposition!

# 1800 CE
# TWO SPORTS ARE
# BETTER THAN ONE England

Football came back in England only in the 1800s and was established in public schools. During that period many attempts were made to define the rules of the game or should we say the 2 games…

In the town of **Eton**, at the most important college of the Kingdom, near Windsor and the Royal Castle, the game was called "the dribbling game" and that is where it developed into the sport that we know as football.

In the town of **Rugby** instead, the game was called "the running game" and it was played mainly with the hands. That's where another sport was born, and that's of course the actual Rugby!

13

**Lord Arthur Kinnaird**

# Shooting Stars

Born in Kensington in 1846 Lord Arthur Kinnaird was **the first football star**!

Founder of the Old Etonians, the football team of Eton college, he was the president of the **English FA (Football Association)** for 33 years as well as the main Board Director of the Barclays Bank.

Incredibly, he holds the current record for most FA CUP finals played (9) and most FA Cup finals won (5). He also scored **the first own goal** in football history, but he never liked to be remembered for that, so this record was hidden for years and it was revealed only in more recent times.

Football was mainly a sport for rich people, playing matches between elite colleges. Arthur was the one who opened the doors of football to the working class and to paid professional players.

In fact, he decided to allow a small club called Darwen to participate in the FA Cup, which was an amateur-only competition, even after the signing of Fergus Suter and Jimmy Love who were the first players to be paid to play.

16

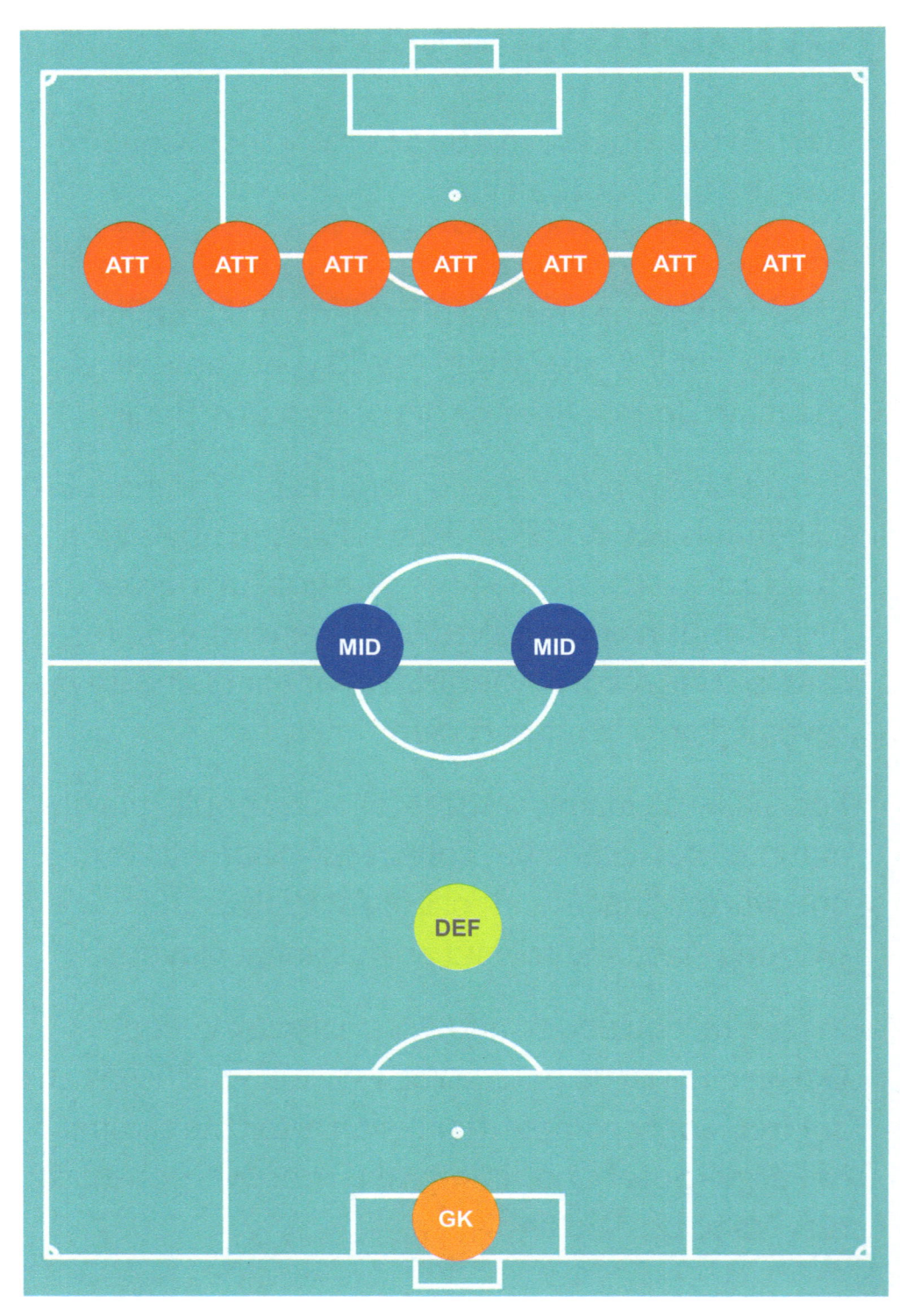

# In the beginning was 1-2-7

Football was an extremely physical game, so in order to have the strongest impact the teams were attacking all together just like a wolf pack.

Dribbling was the most preferred style, players were mainly dribbling and kicking the ball forward.

Today we still witness this ancient strategy during children's matches, where everyone is chasing the ball all over the pitch and it gets very difficult to understand what's going on!

Slowly but surely most teams and players will begin to understand the importance of positioning, which is something that all children eventually will learn at training and by playing matches.

# OPENING MATCH at Olive Grove.

### MONDAY, SEPTEMBER 12th, 1887.

## THE WEDNESDAY v. BLACKBURN ROVERS

### BLACKBURN TEAM.

*Right Wing.*      *Goal.*      *Left Wing.*

H. Arthur.

Jos. Beverley.    A. Chadwick.

Jos. Heyes.    John Barton.    Jas. H. Forrest.

S. Douglas.   N. Walton.   R. Rushton.   L. H. Heyes.   J. Berisford.

### WEDNESDAY TEAM.

J. Smith.

F. Thompson.    J. Hudson.

E. Brayshaw.    W. Betts.    A. Beckett.

H. Winterbottom.   G. Waller.   T. E. B. Wilson.   T. Cawley.   W. Mosforth.

*Umpires* —T. B. MITCHELL; H. ELLIS.    *Referee*—J. C. CLEGG.

# 2-3-5
# "The Pyramid"

Thanks to Fergus Suter, who is still recognised as the first professional footballer, and other football pioneers, the game developed further with new ideas such as **passing** and **moving into space.**

First hints of Tiki Taka?

Not just yet, although teams started to find more clever ways to break through the opposition.

A great innovation was to have one or two strong players, who would have good passing skills, vision, and experience, to be positioned in defence and in the middle of the pitch to circulate the ball better and to set up the forwards to score easily and frequently.

The poster on the left is advertising a football match between two of the oldest clubs in England in 1887, and it shows the teams' lineups displayed in the formations that they were expected to play.

# 20

**LEFT WINGER**

**CENTRE FORWARD**

**RIGHT WINGER**

**INSIDE FORWARD**

**INSIDE FORWARD**

**LEFT HALFBACK**

**CENTRE HALFBACK**

**RIGHT HALFBACK**

**FULL BACK**

**FULL BACK**

**GK**

Goal! • © 2023 Enrico Pomarico

# The Metodo (2-3-2-3)

Devised by Vittorio Pozzo, this new system led Italy to win the World Cup in 1934 and 1938.

More players in the midfield made the defence stronger and the attack was supported with faster counter-attacks.

2-5-3 was and still is nowadays the formation for the Calcio Balilla, the table football game, also known as the Kick!

CENTRE
FORWARD
LEFT
WINGER
RIGHT
WINGER
INSIDE
FORWARD
INSIDE
FORWARD
LEFT
HALFBACK
RIGHT
HALFBACK
FULL
BACK
FULL
BACK
FULL
BACK
GK

# WM

During the 1920s and 1930s, most clubs in England would use the WM.

This formation was invented by Arsenal's coach Herbert Chapman who finally introduced a centre-back to mark the opposition's striker.

No other club was as successful as his team because the strategy was functional to his own players such as Alex James, one of the first playmakers in football history.

This system was called WM because the positioning of the players formed the shape of those two letters.

The WM was the base for other systems that were developed and used in the future, just applying some slight changes to it: for example, aligning the 4 in the middle would make it a 3-4-3, turning the M upside down and making it WW like the Hungarian coach Marton Bukovi did, or making it very compact and defensive to give birth to the notorious "Catenaccio".

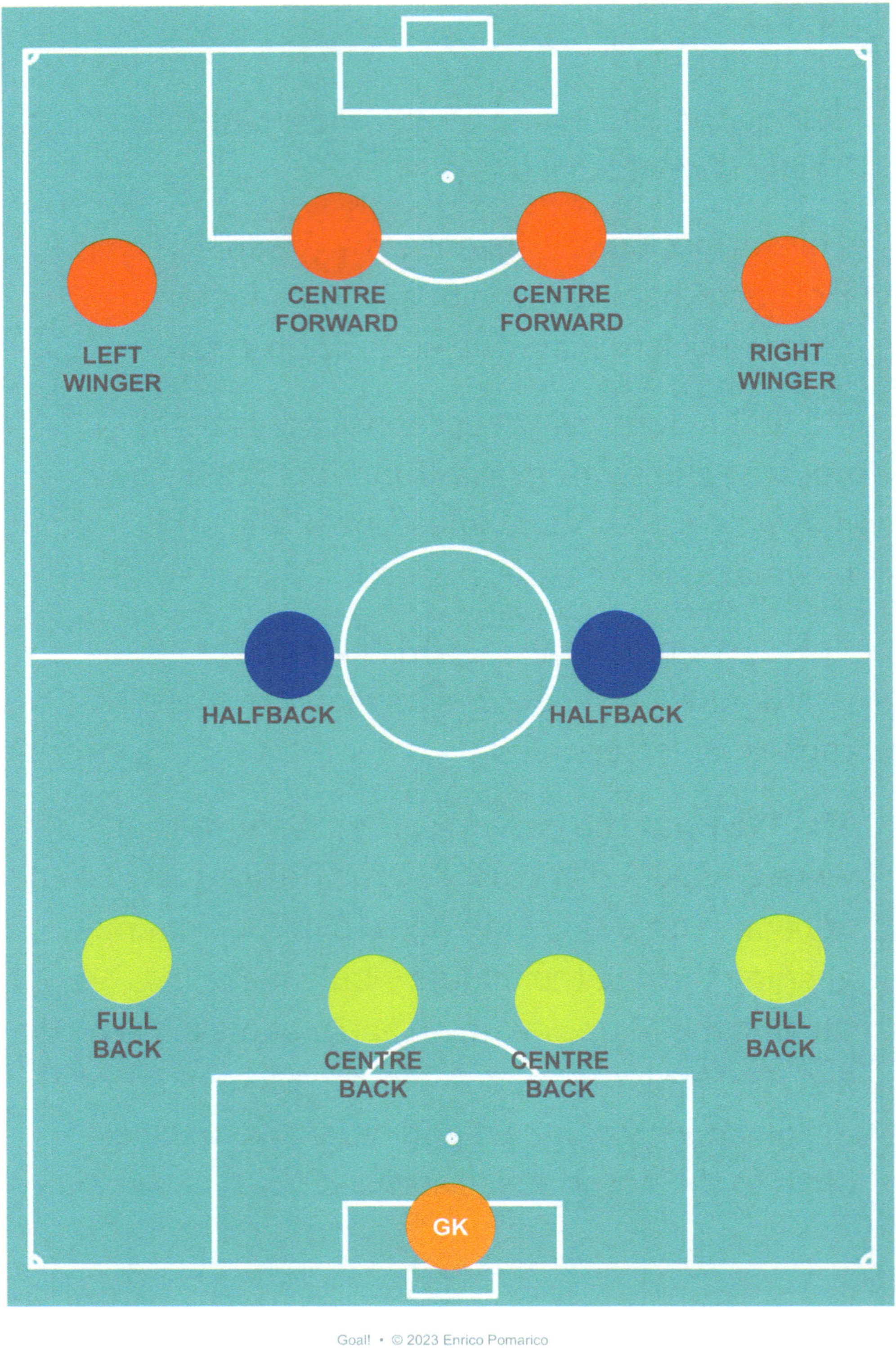
CENTRE
FORWARD
CENTRE
FORWARD
LEFT
WINGER
RIGHT
WINGER
HALFBACK
HALFBACK
FULL
BACK
FULL
BACK
CENTRE
BACK
CENTRE
BACK
GK

# 4-2-4 and the Ginga

There were other attempts to get both defence and attack stronger, one of them was the 4-2-4. Coming from the Hungarian school of Gusztav Sebes, coach of the Mighty Magyars in the 1950s (Olympic champions, European champions, and World Cup runner-up), it was also very successful in Brazil.

4-2-4 was used at the Brazilian club Santos and subsequently adopted by the Brazil national team, both led by the great Pelé. During Pelé's long career, the Brazilian side won the World Cup in 1958, in 1962, and in 1970 thanks to the traditional playing style called Ginga which he used in perfect harmony with Didi, Vavá and Garrincha.

Ginga, meaning "swing" or "sway", is the triangular side steps that Capoeira fighters/dancers use to deceive and trick the opponent. Capoeira is an ancient martial art used by slaves as training to fight by pretending to dance. In football Ginga is playing beautifully (Joga Bonito) by using a lot of flair and skills, especially with the ball in the air. Stunning footwork and acrobatics!

**Johan Cruyff**

# Totaal Voetbal

"Total Football" is a tactical theory in which any outfield player can take over the role of any other teammate (except for the goalkeeper which is a very specialised position) to retain the team's structure.

It was made famous by the Netherlands national football team when reaching the final of the 1974 FIFA World Cup. First created by Rinus Michels, who was awarded the Coach of the Century for his successful career and innovative ideas, it was then developed further by his pupil and best player Johan Cruyff at Ajax, Barcelona, and the Netherlands National team.

Throughout the years it became the signature style of play at Ajax and everywhere in the Netherlands, and also at Barcelona where a young Pep Guardiola was learning the art of coaching whilst playing as central midfielder.

This method has been kept alive in the Dutch coaching philosophy as kids are rotating positions each week up to 16 years old in order to be able to play every role.

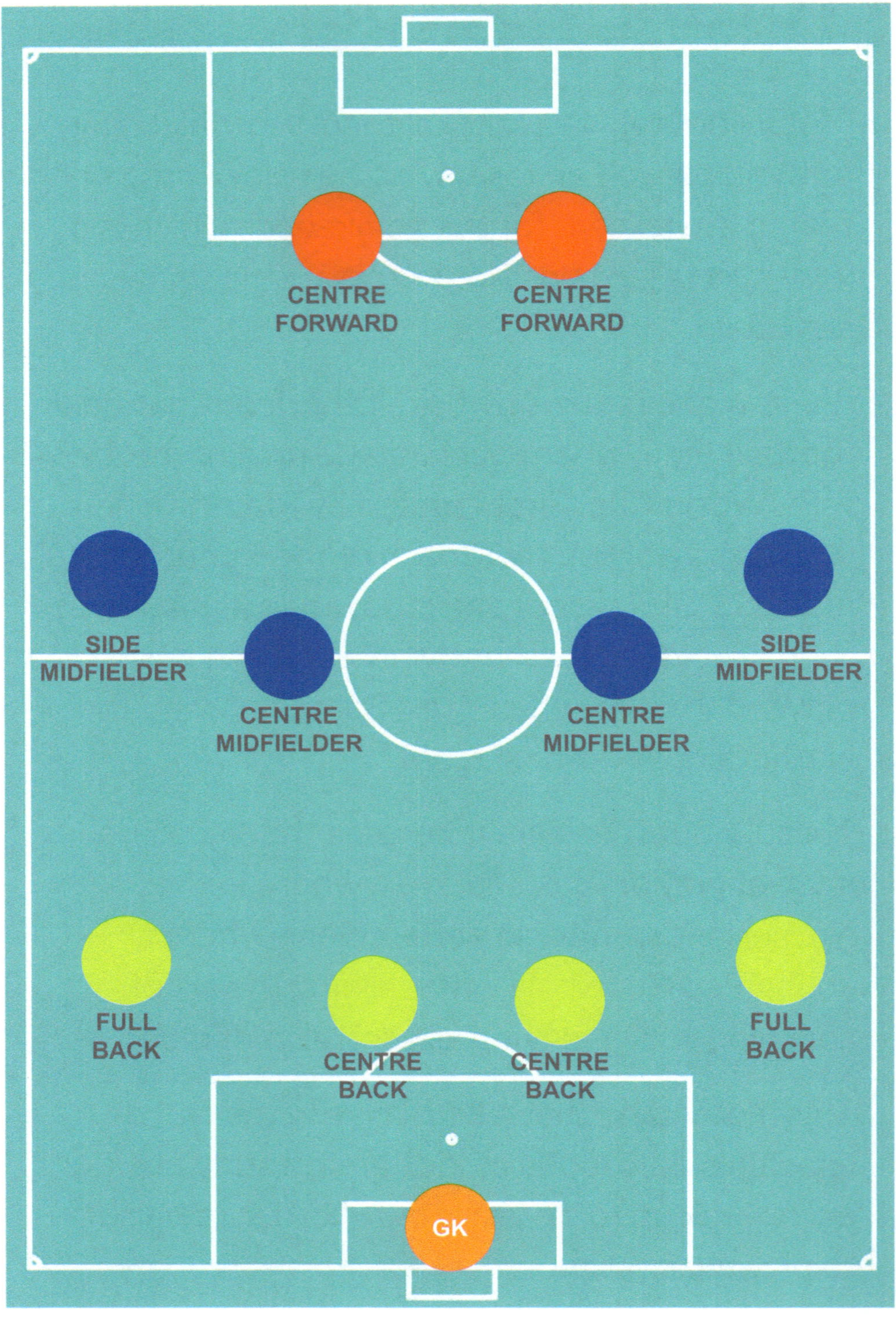
CENTRE
FORWARD
CENTRE
FORWARD
SIDE
MIDFIELDER
CENTRE
MIDFIELDER
CENTRE
MIDFIELDER
SIDE
MIDFIELDER
FULL
BACK
CENTRE
BACK
CENTRE
BACK
FULL
BACK
GK

# 4-4-2

The most balanced formation in modern football and of course the most popular of all time.

Arrigo Sacchi first, and then Fabio Capello, won everything in Italy, in Europe, and in the World with AC Milan using this formation. During that period, this historical club featured some of the finest quality players such as Van Basten, Gullit, Rijkaard, Baresi, Maldini, Ancelotti, Weah, and more.

The offside trap became a powerful weapon to frustrate and defeat opponents like never before.

Also Manchester United was quite an unbeatable team guided by Sir Alex Ferguson with his perfect management skills and stellar signings such as Giggs, Beckham, Cristiano Ronaldo, Schmeichel, Cantona, Rooney and many more.

The 4-4-2 became the FRAME to define each player's position on the pitch and the BASE for every other formation. In fact, by moving a player or two up or down to another line it would transform into 4-3-3, 4-5-1, 3-5-2, 3-4-3, and so on.

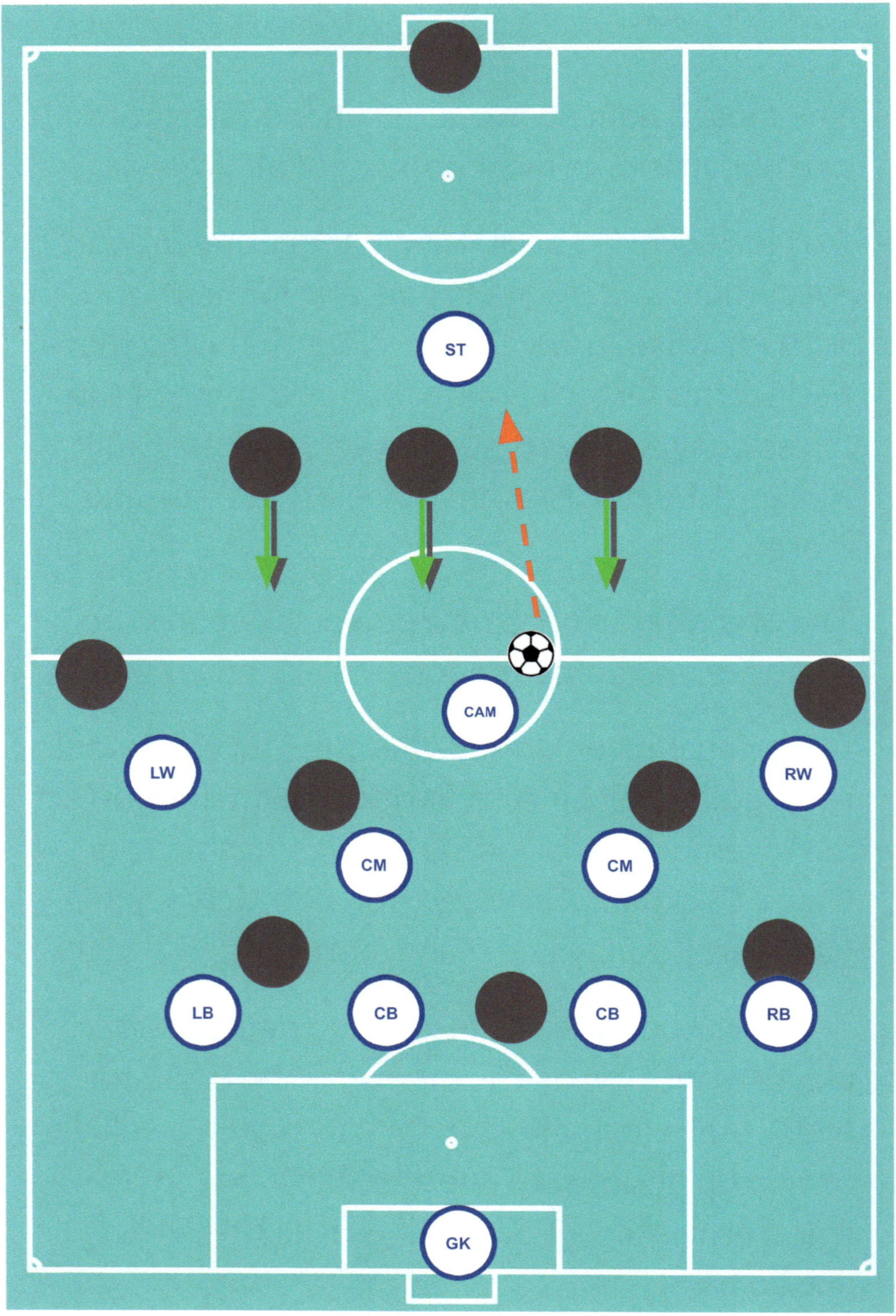
ST
CAM
LW
RW
CM
CM
LB
CB
CB
RB
GK

# The Offside

To avoid the so-called "goal hanging", the offside rule was introduced in 1863. It forced the attacking players not to stand beyond at least 3 players of the defending team (including the goalkeeper).

In 1925, it was adjusted to 2 players including the goalkeeper (the current rule) which practically means not standing beyond the last defender.

The official rule says:
*"A player is in an offside position if any of their body parts, except the hands and arms, are in the opponent's half of the pitch and closer to the opponent's goal line than both the ball and the second-last opponent (the last opponent is usually, but not necessarily, the goalkeeper)."*

If the player in offside receives the ball or even interferes with the action, the sideline referee would raise the flag and the referee would blow the whistle for a foul and a free kick to be taken in the place where the player was spotted in offside.

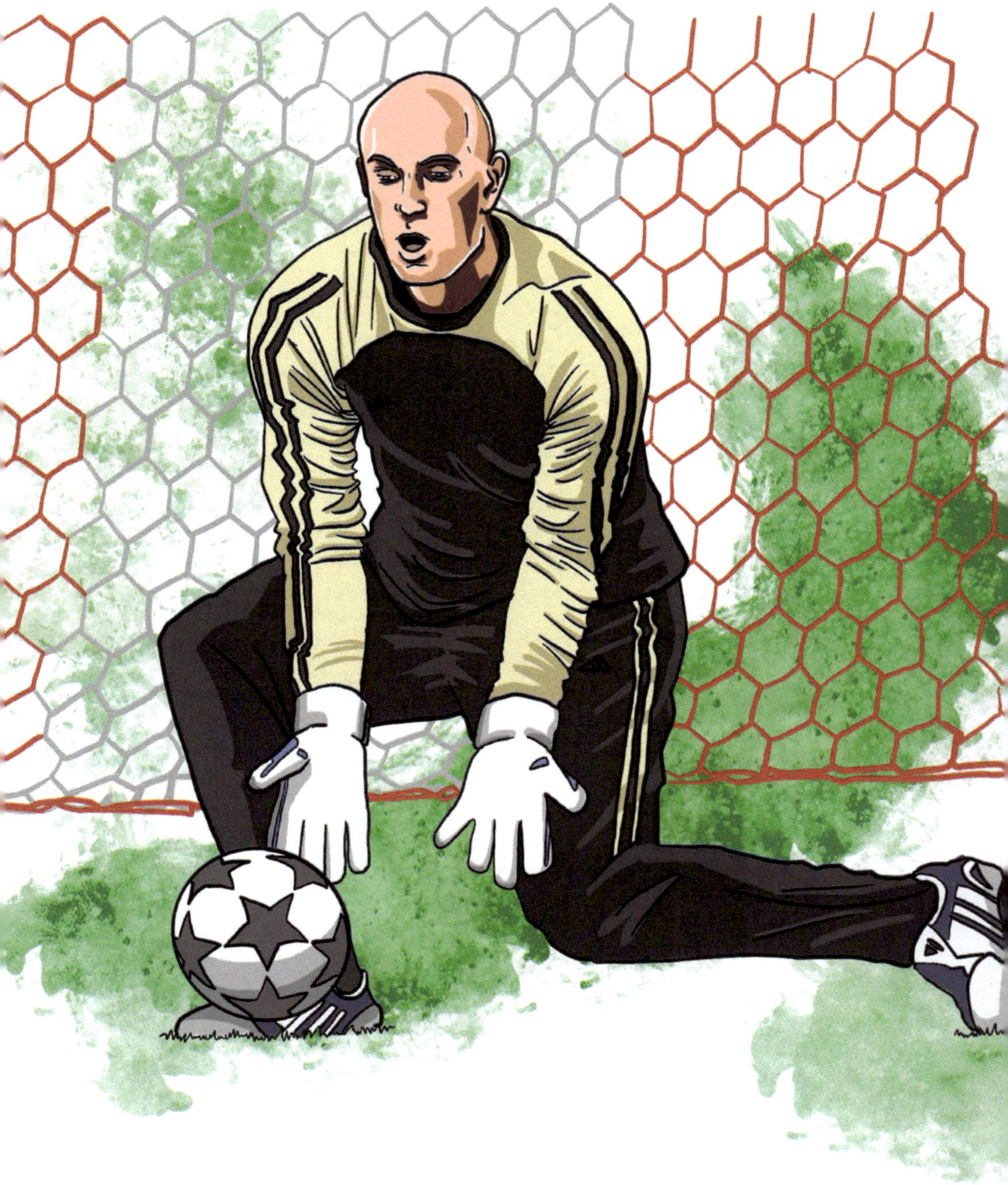

# The back pass rule

In 1992, a new rule was introduced: goalkeepers are no longer allowed to pick up the ball with their hands when the ball is intentionally passed to them by a teammate with a foot pass. In 1997, the new rule was extended also to hand throw-ins.

This rule changed the game in positive ways: it made the game faster, forced goalkeepers to practice playing with the feet, encouraged teams playing from the back, defenders to improve their passing skills and most importantly it reduced drastically dull play and time wasting.
It was very common to use this dull play strategy to make the time pass when a team was happy with the score, passing the ball back and forth with the goalkeeper was just too boring and somehow unfair at times.

Fun fact: during the World Cup of Italy in 1990, the Irish goalkeeper Bonner managed to waste 6 minutes only by dribbling and picking the ball back in his hands continually! This is also no longer allowed because, after the introduction of this rule, goalkeepers can drop the ball and pick it up with their hands only once.

# Balls too have evolved!

### A long time ago...

Imagine heading or making a save with these footballs...
"Free kick, who wants to be in the wall?"

### ... to nowadays

Nike Flight, 2021
The most advanced aerodynamics technology ever known,
born as the result of:
1,700 lab hours
800 footballers testing
68 iterations
1 robotic leg

# Let's take a look at the World Cup balls

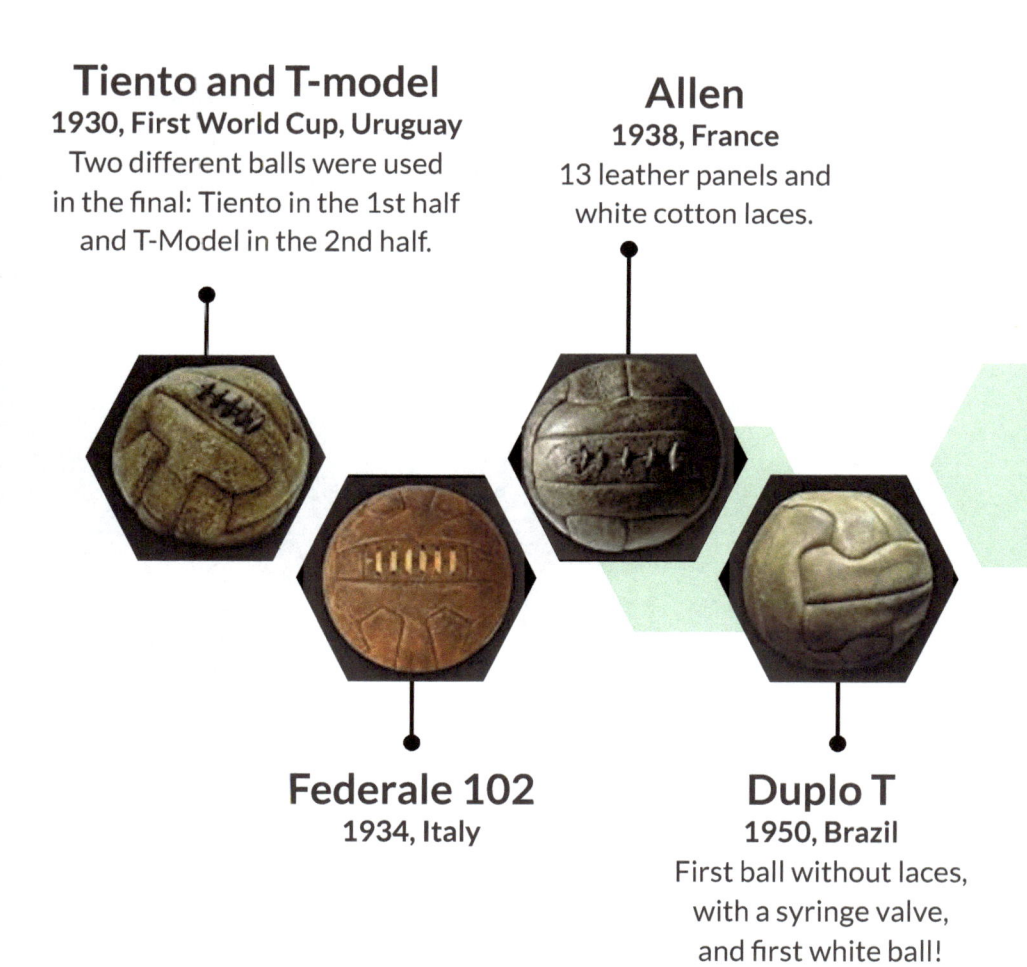

**Tiento and T-model**
1930, First World Cup, Uruguay
Two different balls were used in the final: Tiento in the 1st half and T-Model in the 2nd half.

**Allen**
1938, France
13 leather panels and white cotton laces.

**Federale 102**
1934, Italy

**Duplo T**
1950, Brazil
First ball without laces, with a syringe valve, and first white ball!

Goal! • © 2023 Enrico Pomarico

### Swiss World Champion
**1954, Switzerland**
First 18 panel ball

### Crack
**1962, Chile**
At the opening match, the referee didn't like it and asked to use a different ball. During that World Cup, many different balls were used.

### Top Star
**1958, Sweden**
Chosen by FIFA officials in a blind test between 102 different balls!

### Challenge 4-Star
**1966, England**
A Slazenger orange ball selected in a blind test by the FA.

### Telstar
**1970, Mexico**
The first football with 32 panels, black and white. Made by Adidas.

### Tango
**1978, Argentina**
This Adidas ball made history because it was used for the following Champions Cup and Olympic Games too.

### Telstar Durlast
**1974, West Germany**
First waterproof ball, coated in polyurethane, it was a lot more resistant!

### Tango España
**1982, Spain**
An improved version of the Tango ball. Partly synthetic, it was the last football made of leather.

Goal! • © 2023 Enrico Pomarico

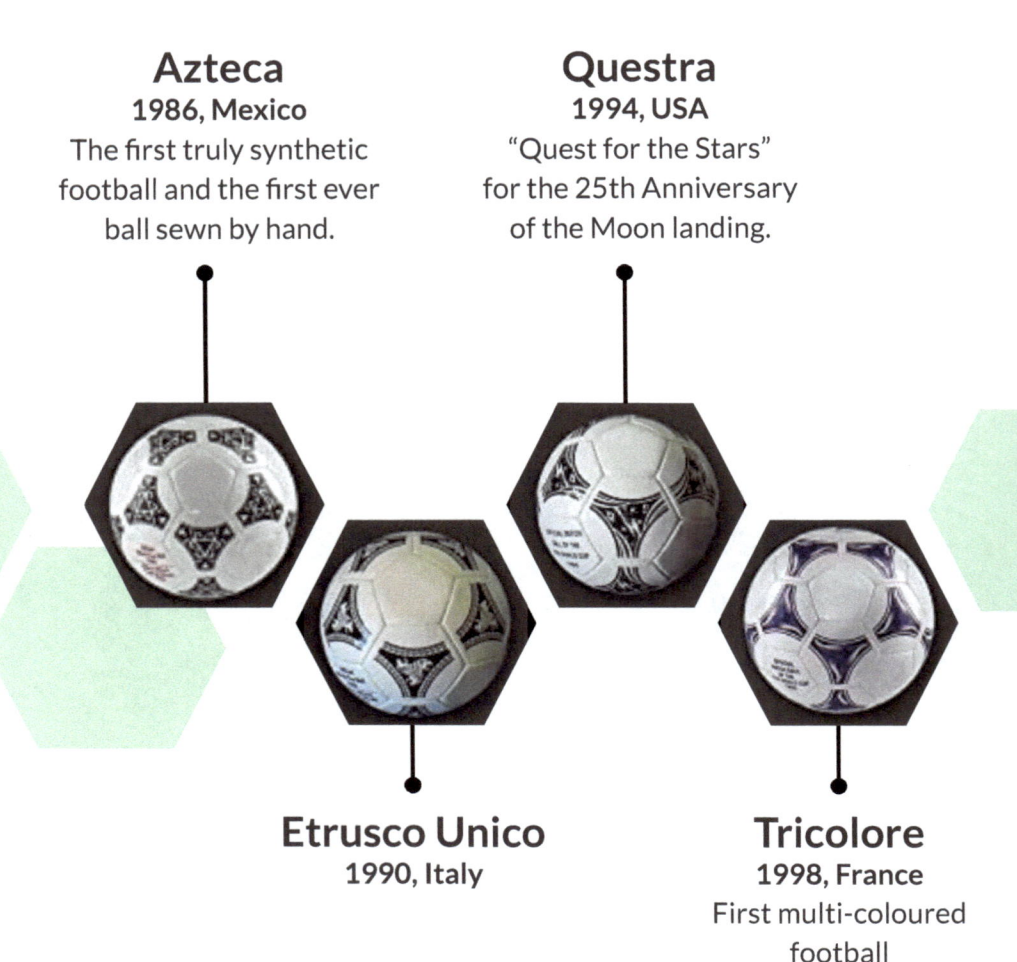

### Azteca
**1986, Mexico**
The first truly synthetic football and the first ever ball sewn by hand.

### Questra
**1994, USA**
"Quest for the Stars" for the 25th Anniversary of the Moon landing.

### Etrusco Unico
**1990, Italy**

### Tricolore
**1998, France**
First multi-coloured football

## Jo'bulani
**2010, South Africa**
The first World Cup on the African continent

## Fevernova
**2002, Korea and Japan**
First football with triangular design

## Telstar 18
**2018, Russia**
Tribute to the Telstar used in Mexico in 1970

## Teamgeist Berlin
**2006, Germany**
Each match had the name of the playing teams printed on the ball. A special golden version was used in the final.

## Brazuca
**2014, Brazil**
The first World Cup ball named by fans

# Chapter 2

# Beyond the pitch: football and society

**The Palmers Munitionettes**

# Girl power

During the First World War (1914-1918), as for other sports and other jobs, **women** took over the football scene.

One of the best teams was "The Palmers Munitionettes" who were working at a munitions factory near Newcastle.

Mary Lyons (sitting in the middle with the ball) was 15 years old, currently the **youngest** player to score a goal for the England senior national team!

The Dick, Kerr & Co. Ladies, usually working at making locomotives and other vehicles, are still to be considered the strongest teams of that time as they had the chance to play against men's teams in the UK and later also successfully touring the USA.

More recently, the French club Olympique Lyonnais built the most dominant women's team of all time. They won the French league 13 times in a row and 6 times the Champions League!

44

# The Christmas Truce of 1914

During war times football had to stop but there was at least one time when football stopped the atrocities of war (with a little help of Christmas magic):

On Christmas Eve of 1914, at the beginning of the First World War, British, French, and German soldiers began to sing carols and soon agreed to 'hold the fire' for the 25th December. The next morning, they crossed trenches, exchanged gifts, and started to play a football game!

This unique event has been documented with pictures, letters, and interviews. Some said that it was only a kick-about, others reported that it was not a match between British & French vs. German soldiers because the teams were mixed!

This is one of the most amazing stories about football as soldiers who had to fight against each other every day came into physical contact to have fun together with our beautiful game!

# Football gets unreal

The very first movie about football was Harry The Footballer, a silent film about a star player kidnapped by the opposition in 1911.

Since, there have been many football-related movies, comedies, documentaries, and dramas. The movie Escape to Victory (1981) is certainly the most iconic of them. It boasts an exceptional cast of renowned actors like Sylvester Stallone and Michael Caine acting and playing football beside all-time football legends such as Pelé, Ardiles, Bobby Moore, and more.

The story is about prisoners in World War II planning their escape during an "unfriendly" exhibition football match vs the Nazist army.

Captain Tsubasa (1983) is the first Japanese cartoon about youth football. It was translated into many languages and soon became one of the most popular cartoons in the world! The series follows the careers of young players up to their adulthood and the apex of their football careers. It has inspired generations with endless battles, incredible shots, and a very romantic scenario.

During the 1980s when computers and video games started to enter people's homes, football video games became very popular: Championship Soccer, International Soccer, Sensible Soccer, Winning Eleven, and more.

In the 1990s, the great rivalry between Pro Evolution Soccer and FIFA began and has accompanied entire generations for decades.

In the 2000s, the debate over which one of the two games is the best was still a big deal!

After the most recent copyright issue that FIFA had with clubs and players, EA Sports decided to make a new independent game called FC.

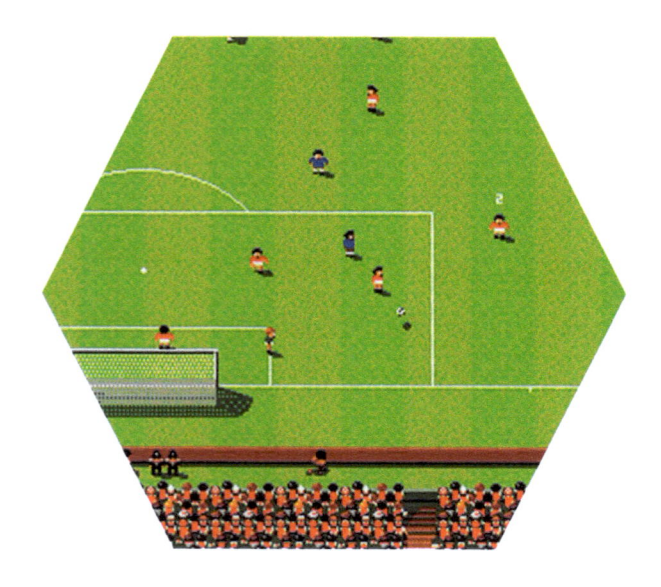

Collecting stickers and cards has become more and more popular over the years.

In the 1970s in Italy, the Panini brothers created collection albums with players' stickers to buy and collect. Their album covers often included the historical bicycle kick by Carlo Parola during a Fiorentina - Juventus of 1950 promptly snapped by Corrado Bianchi, a war photographer borrowed to football.

Throughout the years, Panini extended the business to several other countries and leagues. Following their successful venture more companies started producing stickers and cards not only of football but of all sports, toys, cartoons, and all sorts of hobbies.

# Most valuable players
## (2023)

|  |  |  |
|---|--------|-------|
| 1 | Erling Haaland | € 180m |
| 2 | Kylian Mbappé | € 180m |
| 3 | Jude Bellingham | € 150m |
| 4 | Vinicius Junior | € 150m |
| 5 | Bukayo Saka | € 120m |
| 6 | Victor Osimhen | € 120m |
| 7 | Jamal Musiala | € 110m |
| 8 | Phil Foden | € 110m |
| 9 | Harry Kane | € 110m |
| 10 | Pedri | € 100m |

Goal! • © 2023 Enrico Pomarico

# The greatest show business

Throughout the years, our beloved game has increasingly become a very profitable business.

In addition to the sale of event tickets, greater forms of income began to affect the game: sponsors, TV rights, merchandise, prizes, betting, and more. The incredibly fast development of the last 50 years has contributed to creating a huge gap between the top teams and all the rest.

Powerful multinationals and Sultans have been purchasing the ownership of football clubs and stadiums to reinvest their capital into football.

In most leagues the strongest teams have established a very durable dominance: Bayern Munich in Bundesliga, Paris Saint-Germain in Ligue 1, Juventus in Serie A, Barcelona and Real Madrid in La Liga. In the Premier League the battles for the title have remained quite open thanks to a more fair distribution of the TV rights which allows smaller teams to keep up with the growth of the top teams and to access UEFA qualification prizes.

# The good players

FIFA and UEFA, both billionaire companies, have several charity projects all over the world, to promote and support football in countries affected by wars, drought, or starvation.

It is their duty to do charity work, as stated in the organisation description, and is also important for their image as well as to bring tax relief.

Many football players, active or retired, have been creating charitable foundations to support children with illnesses or in poverty.

These projects are mostly heartful genuine gestures; indeed most players come from humble or difficult backgrounds and they often dedicate their time and the money they earned in football to help communities where they grew up or experiencing similar struggles.

Some great examples are Didier Drogba, Nwankwo Kanu, David Beckham, Rio Ferdinand, Jermain Defoe, Vinicius Junior, Cristiano Ronaldo, and too many more to mention.

## Marcus Rashford

In 2020, **Marcus Rashford** received an MBE award in the UK, together with huge respect and recognition from the wider audience for stepping up in a very determined battle with the government to keep distributing free meals to families during the school closures due to the Covid-19 pandemic lockdown.

# Racism in football

Racism and other forms of discrimination are by far the biggest plague of humanity, which have caused death, suffering, and disparities of treatment and development in every continent. Sadly, racial abuse and discrimination have always existed in football too.

Throughout the years many players have challenged the establishment, the federations, the club's boards, and ultimately the supporters directly. For decades the opportunities and the treatment have not been fair or equal.
In recent years, the football organisations have implemented improvements on their side, but unfortunately at the same time, the racial abuses from the supporters in the stadium and on social media have been unprecedentedly escalating, to the great shock and disgust of the majority of the football lovers and the whole society.

Kick It Out, No Room For Racism and other initiatives supported by players of African and Caribbean descent (and not only) have been trying hard to tackle this problem in collaboration with the authorities and the federations.

**Let's kick racism out of the game all together!** If you experience, see or hear anything that is not right the best thing to do is to report it to anyone whom you trust.

# Hooligans
# (No more violence!)

"Panem et Circenses" ("Give them bread and circuses and they will never revolt") once said the Ancient Roman politician Marcus Tullius Cicero. Meaning that sporting events help distract people from politics and everyday life.

There have been many episodes of sports crowd violence throughout the whole of football history.

The pride of supporting the team that represents one's town, city, region, or country, a strong sense of belonging mixed with the anger of losing, perhaps against a rival team, perhaps not deservedly, often led men to argue and fight.

Eventually, these men got organised in groups leading gigantic fights against groups supporting rival teams and against the authorities trying to stop them.

In the 1970s and 1980s, this phenomenon reached its peak as the frustration brought by difficult social and economic conditions added anger and upset to the popular classes.

It was called Hooliganism in the UK and the same name was adopted everywhere in the World.

Heavy punishments for this crime, together with better stadiums and infrastructures, have helped solve the issue in the UK – although Hooligan firms still exist and occasionally arrange fights in the backstreets or at each other's pubs.

Unfortunately, in many other countries around the World, this problem is very much alive, where ignorance and poverty are taking over, and violence is keeping families with children away from sporting events.

# It's all for us: the fans!

All the financial business and the show business existing around football, it's all for us, the fans: billions of people, who love the game so much to pay for tickets, TV licenses, and merchandise.

All the competitions, leagues, cups, local and international, the intricacy of arranging the calendars for all the fixtures, all the logistics to make it happen, home and away, it's all for us, the fans: billions of people who are demanding it, as often as possible.

All the tactics, the development of the game, the hard and consistent training, the work of science and medicine to support the athletes, all the employees working day and night in all the clubs and companies all around the world, it's all for us the fans: to make the game more interesting, more competitive, more beautiful for us to enjoy it more and more.

All for us, the fans, a short term for fanatics.

We are the ones watching, reading, screaming, praying, cheering, protesting, traveling, buying, complaining, supporting, celebrating, and passing it on to the next generation.

We are the ones who love our teams, our players, our clubs, and our nations so much that we have to show it at all costs with our actions. But love is a powerful thing and with power comes great responsibility. Our passion for the game doesn't have to be excessive, it must not overcome reality, and it must not cause pain to others. Let's enjoy the beautiful game rather than ruining it!

We love to see parents taking their children to the stadium, to breathe the match day atmosphere, enjoy the street food, see thousands of people sharing the same feelings… and enjoy the choreographies, the singing, the anthems, the warm-up, being so close to it, watching our favourite players in action, not on the screen but in real life.

Such a wonderful experience!

60

# Chapter 3

# Organisations and competitions

Slovenia

Japan

Football is everywhere in the world, no matter the geographical location or the weather conditions...

**Switzerland**

**Oman**

Goal! • © 2023 Enrico Pomarico

🏳️ **211 nations**

🏟️ **4,720 stadiums**

🥇 **40,000 clubs**

🏃 **265 million players**

# FIFA

## Fédération Internationale de Football Association

FIFA (founded in 1904) controls, organises and promotes international football, and its competitions.

It also supports approx. 100 football-related social projects all around the world.

The trophy represents Niké (pronounced as nee-keh), the ancient Greek goddess of victory.

# The birth of the World Cup

Football was included for the first time in the 1908 Olympic Games in London.

In 1930, FIFA president Jules Rimet organised the first world cup, hosted and won by Uruguay. The competition was called the **Jules Rimet Trophy**. It became officially the **FIFA World Cup** only in 1974.

It is played every 4 years in a different hosting country that receives funds for building and upgrading sports, transport, and hospitality facilities. In the beginning, this tournament was invitational so only the nations who were invited could participate, and the number of teams was down to the countries who could afford to travel to another continent to join. Later the number of participants expanded to 24, then 32, and finally 48. Now, there are so many countries willing to participate that FIFA had to structure an intricate system of smaller continental qualifying rounds to determine the final 48 nations.

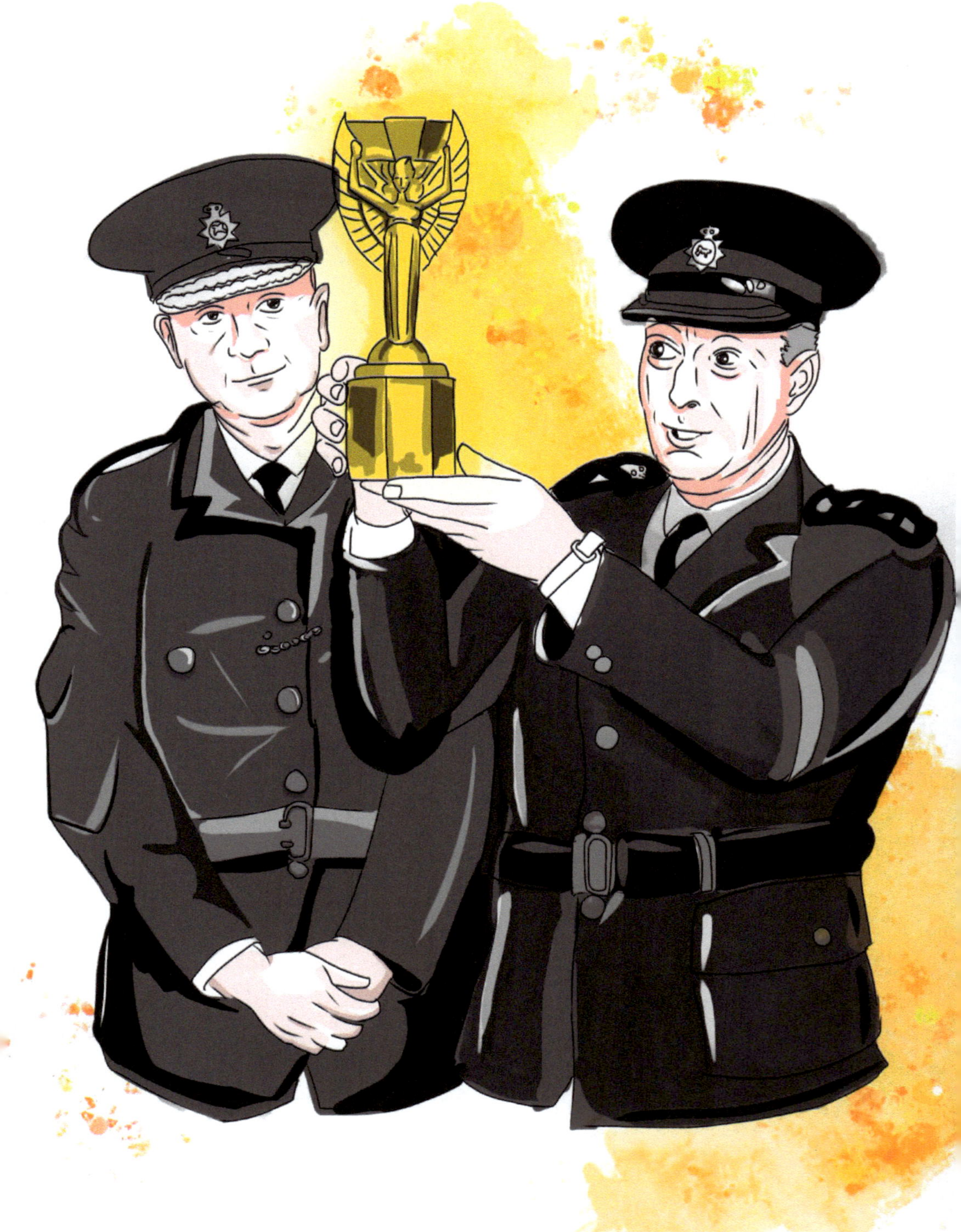

# Pickles the hero

In 1966, four months before the World Cup in England, the trophy was stolen during an exhibition at the Westminster Central Hall.

It was found a week later by a dog called Pickles. The tournament was won by England for the first and only time in history.

Four years later, Brazil was given the honour of keeping the cup forever after winning it for the 3rd time. A new trophy was designed, slightly different, for the following editions of the World Cup, which is still the current one.

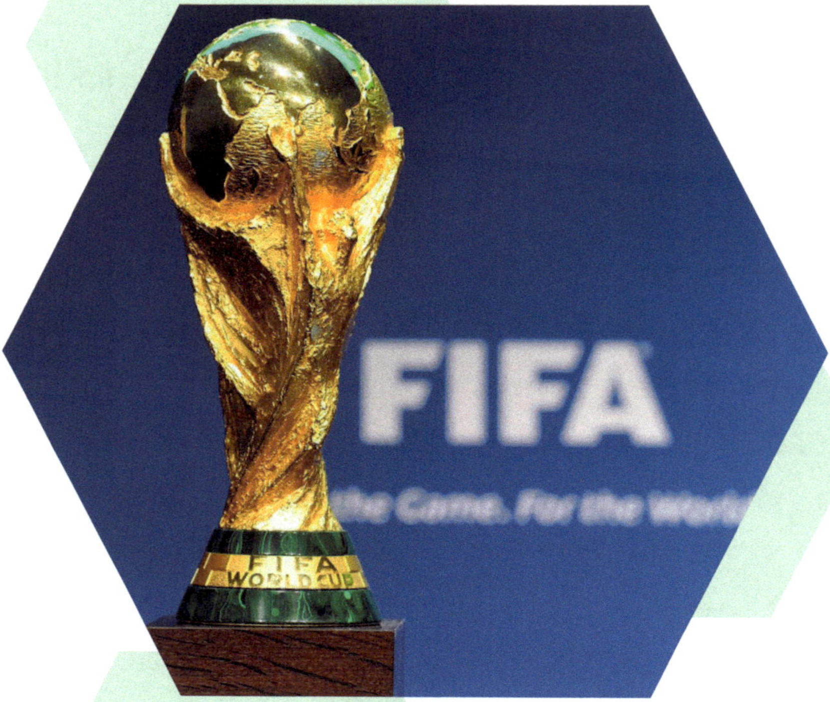
FIFA
FIFA WORLD CUP

# Nations that won the World Cup

| Nation | Number of wins | When |
|---|---|---|
| Brazil 🇧🇷 | 🏆🏆🏆🏆🏆 | 1958, 1962, 1970, 1994, 2002 |
| Italy 🇮🇹 | 🏆🏆🏆🏆 | 1934, 1938, 1982, 2006 |
| Germany 🇩🇪 | 🏆🏆🏆🏆 | 1954, 1974, 1990, 2014 |
| Argentina 🇦🇷 | 🏆🏆🏆 | 1978, 1986, 2022 |
| Uruguay 🇺🇾 | 🏆🏆 | 1930, 1950 |
| France 🇫🇷 | 🏆🏆 | 1998, 2018 |
| England 🏴󠁧󠁢󠁥󠁮󠁧󠁿 | 🏆 | 1966 |
| Spain 🇪🇸 | 🏆 | 2010 |

**Willie**
England, 1966

**Juanito**
Mexico, 1970

**Tip & Tap**
Germany, 1974

**Gauchito**
Argentina, 1978

**Naranjito**
Spain, 1982

**Pique**
Mexico, 1986

**Ciao**
Italy, 1990

**Strike**
USA, 1994

**Footix**
France 1998

**Spherix**
Japan, 2002

**Goleo VI**
Germany, 2006

**Zakumi**
South Africa, 2010

**Fuleco**
Brazil, 2014

**Zabivaka**
Russia, 2018

**La'Eeb**
Qatar, 2022

Goal! • © 2023 Enrico Pomarico

# Qatar 2022

In 2022 the World Cup took place in Qatar, a tiny country in the Middle East with no football history. This was decided in 2010 by FIFA to please very important sponsors and generous investors. They had to build 5 ultra modern stadiums, plus all the facilities and the infrastructure to welcome this huge event.

This decision caused discussions and criticism for the concerns regarding human rights, especially for the way migrant workers (many of them died during the building works), women, and the LGBT community are treated in Qatar.

Another reason for debate was that for the first time in history the World Cup happened during winter (because summer in the Middle East reaches temperatures of 45°C) so all the club competitions had to be paused for 2 months to allow the tournament to take place.

Nevertheless, the show on the pitches was beautiful as always and Argentina won the so-much-awaited 3rd title which was the ultimate achievement for Messi and his teammates.

Alex Morgan

Abby Wambach

# FIFA Women's World Cup and Women's Football

The FIFA Women's World Cup is taking place every four years since 1991. The USA is the most successful team with 4 titles, followed by Germany with 2, Spain, Norway, and Japan with 1.

In the last two decades, women's football has been rapidly growing. The top clubs have been investing in developing this sector, from the youth academy branch to the signing of talented players from all over the world.

This also happened thanks to the big event (the World Cup) being televised, awakening the attention of the media and many girls' dreams who would otherwise hide their passion for football.

However, there is a long way to go for women's football to reach the visibility, financial interest, and support it deserves. Several footballer activists are raising awareness about gender equality, in terms of objectives, wages, respect, and more. The battle is on!

# Each continent has its own Football Federation

where national teams are also competing in **Continental Championships,** usually scheduled 2 years apart from the World Cup to allow the scheduling of qualifier rounds as well as friendly exhibitions.

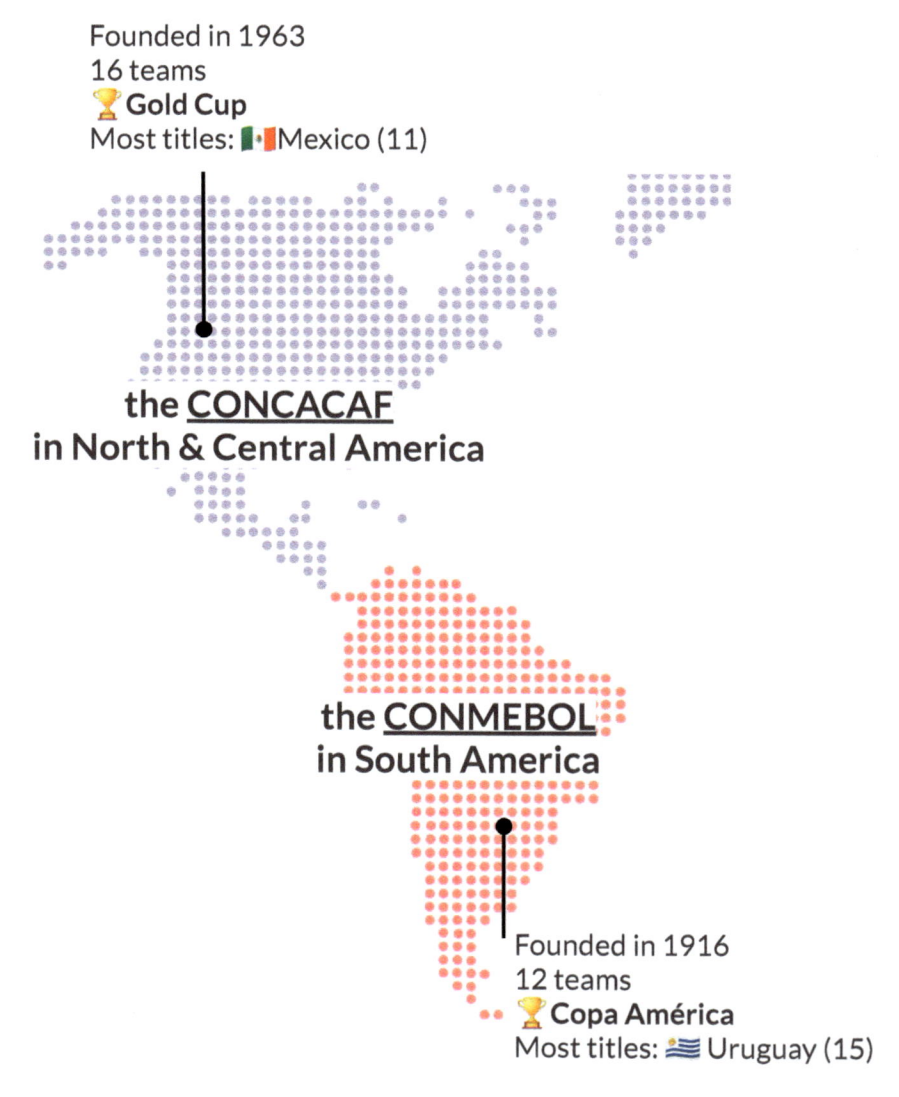

Founded in 1963
16 teams
🏆 Gold Cup
Most titles: 🇲🇽 Mexico (11)

**the CONCACAF**
in North & Central America

**the CONMEBOL**
in South America

Founded in 1916
12 teams
🏆 Copa América
Most titles: 🇺🇾 Uruguay (15)

Goal! • © 2023 Enrico Pomarico

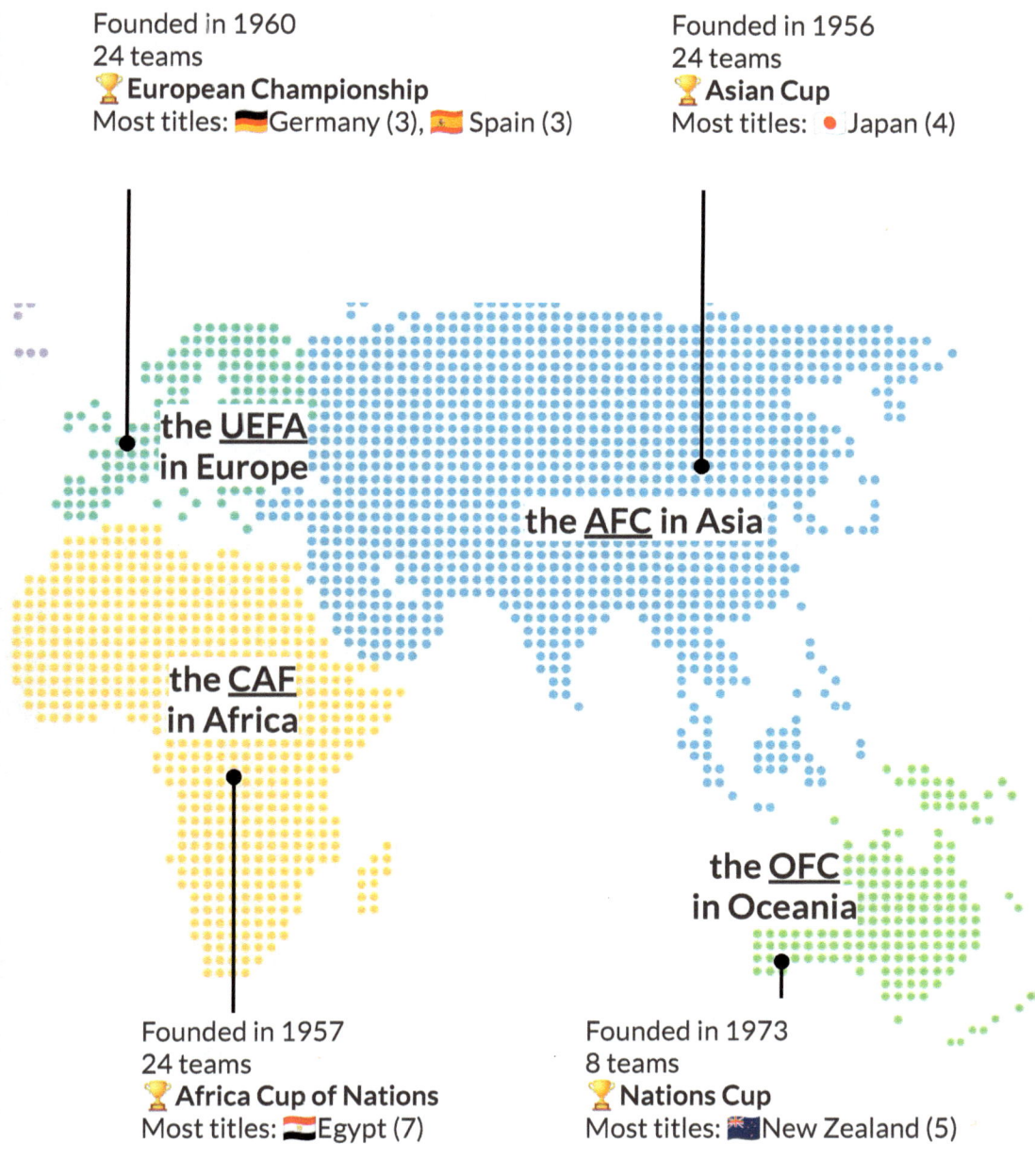

Founded in 1960
24 teams
🏆 **European Championship**
Most titles: 🇩🇪 Germany (3), 🇪🇸 Spain (3)

Founded in 1956
24 teams
🏆 **Asian Cup**
Most titles: 🔴 Japan (4)

the **UEFA** in Europe

the **AFC** in Asia

the **CAF** in Africa

the **OFC** in Oceania

Founded in 1957
24 teams
🏆 **Africa Cup of Nations**
Most titles: 🇪🇬 Egypt (7)

Founded in 1973
8 teams
🏆 **Nations Cup**
Most titles: 🇳🇿 New Zealand (5)

Goal! • © 2023 Enrico Pomarico

# Club competitions

Each country has its own Football Federation which is responsible for the organisation and running of the national leagues for clubs. In each country, there is a top division, such as the Premier League, Serie A, La Liga, Bundesliga, and several lower divisions down to regional competitions.

Every season is played usually from August to May, with some breaks to allow the best players to take part in training and matches with their national teams. Leagues and their lower divisions are composed of 16-20 clubs. During a season, each club has to face all the other clubs twice. Each win gives the club 3 points, the draw gives only 1 point and the loss gives 0.

Based on those points, at the end of the season, the clubs that are at the top of the top division table will qualify to play against clubs from neighbouring countries in the next season. The clubs at the bottom of the table (usually 3) will be relegated to the lower divisions. In the lower divisions, the clubs at the top of the table will be promoted to play in the above division.

Clubs are also involved in national Cups. These parallel tournaments have a knockout structure and all clubs of all divisions participate. At the bottom of these Cup's knockout tables, there are clubs from lower divisions clashing between them to get the chance to play against the top division teams that are joining at a later stage.

For clubs and players of lower divisions, the national Cups are very important as they may bring lifetime opportunities in terms of image returns, sponsors, ticket sales, and contracts for the players. Occasionally, small town clubs manage to host at their home grounds some of the best players in the world. This is something really magic that keeps everyone's dreams alive! The greatest example is the FA Cup in England, as it brings to life amazing stories and surprising results year after year!

Clubs and players of the top clubs of the highest divisions in each country are involved in matches for the League Cup, and continental competitions such as the Champions League, and Europa League. This allows them very little time to rest and to prepare for each match as they practically play every 3 days non-stop.

|  | Association Club Coefficients | Number clubs qualified in Champions, Europa and Conference Leagues |
| --- | --- | --- |
| England 🏴󠁧󠁢󠁥󠁮󠁧󠁿 | 91.678 | 8 |
| Spain 🇪🇸 | 78.489 | 8 |
| Italy 🇮🇹 | 74.569 | 7 |
| Germany 🇩🇪 | 71.909 | 7 |
| Netherlands 🇳🇱 | 56.500 | 5 |
| France 🇫🇷 | 54.831 | 6 |
| Portugal 🇵🇹 | 49.316 | 6 |
| Belgium 🇧🇪 | 40.400 | 5 |
| Türkiye 🇹🇷 | 34.850 | 4 |
| Scotland 🏴󠁧󠁢󠁳󠁣󠁴󠁿 | 32.250 | 5 |
| Austria 🇦🇹 | 30.800 | 5 |

# UEFA Ranking

The high-ranking countries can qualify for up to 4 clubs. In the low-ranking countries, the winning clubs go through qualifier rounds to access the Champions League.

These values are updated every year depending on clubs' performances in European competitions.

UEFA also includes countries that are not exactly in Europe like Russia, Azerbaijan, Kazakhstan, and Israel, for a total of 55 countries!

That's why qualifier rounds are necessary. Low-ranking clubs and clubs of low-ranking countries must play a mini tournament made of 3-4 rounds to finally be able to access the Champions League or the Europa League.

The clubs are playing each other twice, home and away, in case of the same total of goals on aggregate they will continue to extra time and penalties.

Recently the "away goals rule", stating that goals scored from the away team would count double in case of a draw, was removed. So finally nobody will ever need to worry about that anymore!

Santiago Bernabéu

# The birth of the UEFA Champions League

**Santiago Bernabéu** is the most important man in Real Madrid's history.
First, he was the striker and the captain of the team. After retiring from playing, he became assistant manager and manager. Then, he was the president of the club for 35 years! Real Madrid's stadium is named in his honour.

In 1955, he created the **European Cup**, whose name changed to **Champions League** in 1992.

The structure of the tournament also changed: based on the ranking certain countries would get more than one club to participate increasing significantly the number of teams (32), so the group stages were introduced (8 groups of 4 teams) before the knockouts.

When Real Madrid won the 1st edition, Santiago Bernabéu created the rule that winners qualify automatically for next year's tournament...
They won it 5 years in a row and 14 times in total.

Goal! • © 2023 Enrico Pomarico

# UEFA Champions League winners

# FIFA Club World Cup winners

| Club | Number of wins | When |
|---|---|---|
| **Real Madrid** 🇪🇸 | 🏆🏆🏆🏆🏆 | 2014, 2016, 2017, 2018, 2022 |
| **Barcelona** 🇪🇸 | 🏆🏆🏆 | 2009, 2011, 2015 |
| **Corinthians** 🇧🇷 | 🏆🏆 | 2000, 2012 |
| **Bayern Munich** 🇩🇪 | 🏆🏆 | 2013, 2020 |
| **São Paulo** 🇧🇷 | 🏆 | 2005 |
| **Internacional** 🇧🇷 | 🏆 | 2006 |
| **Milan** 🇮🇹 | 🏆 | 2007 |
| **Manchester United** 🏴󠁧󠁢󠁥󠁮󠁧󠁿 | 🏆 | 2008 |
| **Internazionale** 🇮🇹 | 🏆 | 2010 |
| **Liverpool** 🏴󠁧󠁢󠁥󠁮󠁧󠁿 | 🏆 | 2019 |
| **Chelsea** 🏴󠁧󠁢󠁥󠁮󠁧󠁿 | 🏆 | 2021 |

# The FIFA Club World Cup

The winners of the Champions League in each continent will compete in the FIFA Club World Cup (formerly known as Intercontinental Cup).

This is the ultimate competition for Clubs to define which is the strongest club in the world.

The tournament consists of a straight knockout stage between 7 teams: the winners of that year's AFC Champions League (Asia), CAF Champions League (Africa), CONCACAF Champions League (North America), Copa Libertadores (South America), OFC Champions League (Oceania) and UEFA Champions League (Europe), along with the host nation's national champions.

# UEFA Europa League winners

# The birth of the UEFA Europa League

In 1960, the UEFA created the **Cup Winners' Cup** to have a tournament between the champions of all domestic cups.

In 1971, the **UEFA Cup** was created for the clubs ranked 2nd and 3rd in each European top league.

In 1999, the Cup Winners' Cup was abolished and merged with the UEFA Cup. From that moment on, all domestic cup winners will qualify for the UEFA Cup together with the 1 or 2 clubs who ended the season just below the clubs who qualified for the Champions League.

The competition was rebranded in 2009 as the UEFA Europa League, structured in a group stage and knockout stage more similar to the Champions League.

Before the rebranding, the finals were played over 2 legs (home and away) but since 1998 finals have been played on a single match in a neutral city selected before the beginning of the competition.

**UEFA Super Cup**
(prev. called European Super Cup)

**UEFA Cup Winners' Cup**

**Champions League**
(prev. called the European Cup)

**UEFA Europa League**

**UEFA Europa Conference League**

# The UEFA Super Cup

The winner of the Champions League and the winner of the UEFA Europa League play a single match for another title called the **UEFA Super Cup.**

Founded in 1972, it was a double-match and it was played between the winner of the European Cup (the old Champions League) and the winner of the Cup Winners' Cup.

This trophy was called the European Super Cup. In 1995, it was renamed UEFA Super Cup following the rebranding of the UEFA.

Real Madrid, Barcelona and AC Milan are the clubs who won it most times (5), followed by Liverpool FC (4), Atletico Madrid (3), Chelsea, Bayern Munich, Juventus, Atletico Madrid, Ajax, Valencia and Anderlecht (2), and a long list of clubs following with 1 title.

Terry McDermott and Radamel Falcao are the only 2 players who scored a hat-trick (3 goals) in this final.

UEFA
CHAMPIONS LEAGUE
UEFA
EUROPA LEAGUE
UEFA
EUROPA CONFERENCE LEAGUE
1
2
3

# The UEFA Europa Conference League

The Conference League is the newest UEFA competition, as it was launched in 2021.

Structured just like the Champions League and Europa League it is practically the 3rd division of European club competitions. The clubs qualifying for the Conference League are those ending the season just below the clubs qualifying for the Europa League.

Interestingly the competition has been created for clubs of lower-ranked leagues therefore the criteria for participation are opposite of the Champion League ones: top-ranked nations have only 1 team, whilst going down the ranking lower-ranked nations will qualify 2 or 3 clubs. They are also joined by 10 teams eliminated in the Europa League playoffs.

The first winner of this competition was Roma managed by José Mourinho. In the second year, West Ham took the trophy to East London for long-awaited celebrations as they had been missing a European title since 1965.

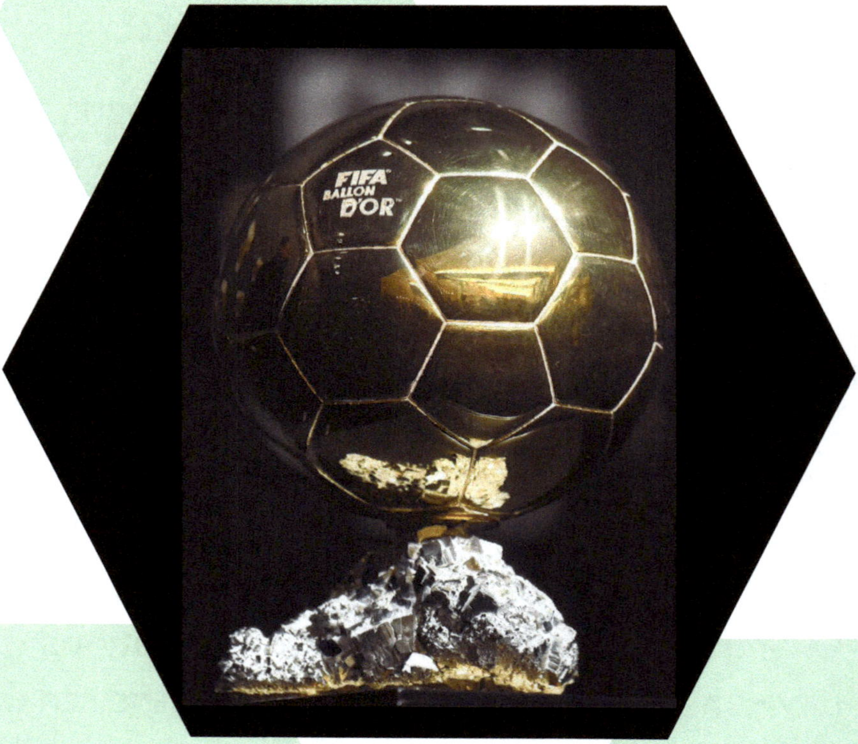
FIFA
BALLON
D'OR

# The Ballon d'Or ("Golden Ball")

The Ballon d'Or is an annual award presented by the French magazine France Football since 1956. In 1991, the FIFA World Player of the Year was created. The 2 awards were merged for 5 years, then were separated again.

The Ballon d'Or remains the most important individual award today because of its tradition and prestige.

France Football introduced the Ballon d'Or Féminin for women's football only in 2018 whilst FIFA started awarding women in 2001.

Between 1956 and 1995 only European footballers playing in Europe could be awarded.

In recent history, Messi and Cristiano Ronaldo have been mostly receiving this award battling each other with goals, trophies, and important sponsorship deals.

Some names for the future? Haaland, Bellingham, Mbappé, Vinicius Jr… only time will tell!

Awards ceremony at Stokey United

# The road to success

To succeed in football, just as for anything else in life or any other sport, it's important to work hard, respect yourself and others, and be disciplined and committed. Practice, fitness, and nutrition are the key elements to reach and maintain appropriate levels, as well as preventing injuries and illnesses.

Football is the biggest dream for most children and can represent the hope of a way out for those born in developing countries, just like Ronaldinho, Sadio Mané and many others.

Each country has different systems in place however the most common distinction in youth football is between grassroots and academic.

In adult football, there are many divisions starting from amateur going up to semi-professional and professional football.

Professional clubs each have their network of talent scouts to discover grassroots players, amateurs, and semi-pro players and bring them on to academic and professional football if they reckon they have talent and potential.

# Chapter 4

# Making history

# Who's the best

**Lionel Messi**

**Cristiano Ronaldo**

Goal! • © 2023 Enrico Pomarico

# player in the world?

*Let's discuss with your friends!*

Help! The world of football is divided in two! Whose side are you on? Here are some clues: Messi had a natural talent whilst Cristiano Ronaldo worked super hard for it. CR7 has scored more goals than Messi but he couldn't do the same things that Messi could do with the ball at his feet.

Messi was awarded 8 Ballon d'Or whilst CR7 has got 5. Cristiano Ronaldo won the European Championship with Portugal whilst Messi won the World Cup with Argentina.

They play slightly different roles so they could even play together in the same team, just imagine how that would work out...
In 2023, at the ages of 36 and 38 when players usually retire, they are still at the top of the game battling for trophies and recognition!

At this point is a matter of personal taste. Watch some videos and some live matches to make up your mind!

# Who's the best

This has been the greatest debate of all time and it's still open! Both Pelé and Maradona are national heroes in Brazil and Argentina and not only...

## Pelé

Pelé symbolised the empowerment of the minorities, alongside other athletes of African & Caribbean descendants in other sports. He is the greatest football icon of all time and is respected as such everywhere in the World!

The things they could do with the football were incredible. The way they could motivate, bring together, and carry along their clubs and nation was an outstanding example of leadership. Their connection with the people shown in every single interview and each goal celebration was proof of their awareness of being heroes.

They won everything in their careers for both clubs and country and yet never were awarded the Ballon d'Or: Pelé because at the time of being an active player, the award was

# player in history?

## Diego A. Maradona

In Napoli (Italy), as well as in Buenos Aires (Argentina), Diego or D10s is idolised like a god: hundreds of paintings, photos, and graffiti are spread across the two cities to pay respect for what he did for the clubs, the cities and for Argentina both in sports achievements and in terms of social revenge.

only for those who played in European leagues, and **Maradona** because he was always against the establishment, never afraid to speak up about serious issues regarding FIFA and UEFA which eventually proved him right.

After all, they were two different kinds of players and played in two different historical periods when football was played in different ways, with different rules, footballs, and boots.

Pelé never played in Europe like Maradona, so it's very difficult, if not impossible, to compare them. We can only admire them!

## Christine Sinclair

The Canadian striker **Sinclair** is the all-time female leading goal scorer. With 190 goals scored for the Canada national team, she holds the record of goals with the national team for both men and women! 14 times winner of the Canada Soccer Player of the Year award, she played and scored in 6 World Cup editions.

## George Weah

**George Manneh Oppong Weah** was the first non-European player and the first and only African player to be awarded the Ballon d'Or. The most significant period of his career was at AC Milan, winning many trophies and scoring incredible goals.

Very popular in his country Liberia, he went into politics and became the President after his football career!

## Gary Lineker

**Gary Lineker** was so much "The Golden Boy" in England. Always kind in manners and elegant with the football, he was awarded the Fair Play Award since he never had a yellow or a red card in his entire career! Now you can recognise him as a journalist presenting many football shows on TV. He scored many goals for clubs and country but he will be also remembered for that time during an Italy 90 World Cup match when he couldn't hold it and decided to poop on the pitch whilst pretending to do some stretching!

Goal! • © 2023 Enrico Pomarico

## Didier Drogba

The most representative football player in the history of Ivory Coast whose importance is recognised in all the African continent, **Didier Drogba** is one of the greatest African players of all time. He played a vital role in bringing peace to his country, which was suffering a terrible 5 years long internal war: in 2007 he asked that the game Ivory Coast vs Madagascar be played in Bouake, the stronghold of the rebels. After the match, which was won also with his goal, he invited the TV cameras into the dressing room and pleaded for the rebels to drop the weapons. This led to an unexpected ceasefire, the end of the war, and peaceful elections!

## Sir Alex Ferguson

One of the greatest managers of all time, **Sir Alex Ferguson** managed Manchester United for 26 years and won 38 trophies! During this period, he launched top players, and legends such as Beckham, Giggs, Rooney, and Cristiano Ronaldo and signed stars like Schmeichel, Cantona, Keane, Van Nistelrooy, and Tevez to name just a few. His role at the club was a lot wider than managing/coaching the team. He had a say in all the decision-making at the club such as the academy, the branding, the food menu, the habits of the players, and even their looks!

## Francesco Totti

Totti was an authentic champion, on and off the pitch. He is considered one of the best footballers in history although he won very few titles and trophies.

The truth is that he did something perhaps even greater than winning cups: he declined a multitude of offers, some shockingly big, from all the top clubs in the world. He had decided to play exclusively for the team of his heart, AS Roma, and so he did.

The celebration of his last match was such an emotional event for football lovers all over the world, not only in Rome, where he'll be forever considered the king.

## Rogério Ceni

The goalkeeper with the most goals scored in history. **Ceni** played for Brazilian club São Paulo FC for 23 years and has also been a manager for his beloved club as well as others. In his 1,257 total appearances, he scored 132 goals (!!!) of which 61 from free kicks, 70 from penalties, and 1 from open play.

Taking set pieces is a very important skill and it doesn't matter what position you play if you are the best at it!

# The Scorpion Kick Save by René Higuita 🦂

**Trick**

One of the most spectacular (and risky!) moves in football history! Goalkeepers are known for being a little bit crazy but **Higuita** went above and beyond: he would just take the ball and start dribbling around leaving the goal unprotected!

He certainly caused some problems to the Colombian national team and all the clubs he played for but watching him play was always worth the price of the ticket!

# The Cuauhteminha by Cuauhtémoc Blanco

**Trick**

Authentic superstar in Mexico, **Blanco** invented this trick to exit the pressure of two or more opponents: block the ball with both feet and jump with it through the tiny space between the opponents! So much fun and original that people decided to call this trick with by first name!

# The Panenka (chip shot) by Antonin Panenka

**Trick**

In 1976, **Panenka** invented the chip shot, which is still widely known as the Panenka shot!
It was the final of the European Championship and Czechoslovakia won against West Germany thanks to this surprising shot. In the "Panenka", the goalkeeper is sure that the shooter will aim at the corners of the goal and instead, the shooter comes up with a soft lob shot in the center of the goal!

# And lots more to explore!

## Find online videos of:

- Zidane's Roulette
- Cruyff's Turn
- Puskas' 'V' Move
- Okocha's Turn
- Zola's Mule Kick
- Quaresma's Trivela
- Infante's Rabona
- Taddei's Aurelio
- Pirlo's Maledetta
- Rivellino's Elastico
- Ronaldinho's Toe Poke
- Free kicks by Roberto Carlos

Every day there are new heroes, new skills, and new amazing stories coming from our beloved beautiful game.
Keep reading, watching, researching, and, of course, most importantly, keep playing!

The story continues...

## Sources

- Wikipedia
- FIFA.com
- Mapsofworld.com
- Independent.co.uk
- 1st-man.com
- Milleworld.com
- captaintsubasa.fandom.com
- Hurriyetdailynews
- Dailymotion
- TheGuardian.com
- TheSun.co.uk
- La Repubblica.it
- FIFAforums.easports.com
- Cbssports.com
- Bleacherreport.com
- UEFA.com
- Footballhistory.com
- Yesterday.uktv.co.uk
- Transfermarkt.co.uk
- BBC.com

## Acknowledgements

*To all the players, staff and board at Stokey United, the club I founded.
To all the players, staff and board at Royal Parthenope FC of which I'm the sporting director and co-founder.*

*To all the players and staff at SSC Napoli of the season 22/23
who made history by giving us the 3rd scudetto after 33 years.
"Io della maglia azzurra so' innamorato…"*

## Special thanks to

*Fluidofinto for his beautiful illustrations,
Sandrine Herbert-Razafinjato for the precious design work,
Ciro-Mael for making me love football even more.*

# Goal!
# The history of football

## by Enrico Pomarico

**ISBN: 9798866762187**
Independently published • © 2023

Printed in Poland
by Amazon Fulfillment
Poland Sp. z o.o., Wrocław